ISLAM RISING

The Middle East and Us

by

Stuart Robinson

Award Winning & Bestselling Author

CHI BOOKS

BY THE SAME AUTHOR

MOSQUES & MIRACLES
Revealing Islam and God's Grace

DEFYING DEATH
Zakaria Botross — Apostle to Islam

TRAVELING THROUGH TROUBLED TIMES
Released from Fear through Faith With Habakkuk

THE PRAYER OF OBEDIENCE

THE PROMISE OF VISION

THE CHALLENGE OF ISLAM

PERSEVERING PRAYER
Growing Your Church Supernaturally

POSITIONING FOR POWER
Kneeling Low in Prayer Standing Tall in God

PRAYING THE PRICE

WHAT OTHERS ARE SAYING ABOUT THIS BOOK ...

"The rise of IS came as a surprise to many, and the reasons for its violent actions are still a mystery to some, particularly politicians. Stuart Robinson is in no doubt—he has done his research and understands why this organization is acting the way that it is. With typical careful background investigation and insightful analysis, Robinson clarifies what some are too afraid to admit about Islamic State. But he moves beyond analysis to providing some practical ways that the common person can respond positively to what could easily become an existential threat to our current existence. A book to be thoroughly recommended."

Dr Bernie Power
Lecturer in Islamic Studies, Melbourne School of Theology, Australia

"What is happening in the house of Islam? And Why? And what should we do about it? As evil tries to advance, God is on the move! In this riveting book, Stuart Robinson calls Christians to get ready to bring in a harvest 'the like of which has never before been seen in human history'."

Rev. Dr Mark Durie
Author and Anglican Pastor, Melbourne, Australia

"Stuart Robinson's "Islam Rising" sets the conflicts of the Middle East in their historic and religious context, so as to assist Christians and Westerners who, due to ignorance of history and of Islam, are finding it difficult to cut through the propaganda and misreporting to make sense of events. His pastor's heart shines through as he draws our attention to the plight of the persecuted. His love of freedom is evident in his concern over rising Islamic influence in the West. Never reactionary, Robinson's response is Biblical, revealing the heart of an evangelist who is excited by the evidence of God at work. This little book will most certainly aid understanding, challenge apathy and inspire hope."

Elizabeth Kendal
Religious Liberty Analyst and Author, Melbourne, Australia
www.elizabethkendal.com

CHI–Books,
PO Box 6462, Upper Mt Gravatt,
Brisbane, QLD 4122, Australia

www.chibooks.org
publisher@chibooks.org

Printed in Australia, United Kingdom and the United States of America.

Also available from: www.bookdepository.co.uk and other outlets like Koorong.com in Australia.

Distribution of eBook version: Amazon Kindle, Apple iBooks, Koorong. com and others like Wesley Owen (UK), Barnes & Nobel NOOK, Sony eReader and KOBO.

Editorial assistance: Anne Hamilton and Geoff Holdway
Cover design: Hadassah Wallis

CONTENTS

INTRODUCTION   1

CHAPTER ONE   No Compromise   3

CHAPTER TWO   Gaza and Israel   7

CHAPTER THREE   Northern Syria and Iraq   13

CHAPTER FOUR   Why is This Happening?   17

CHAPTER FIVE   Our Response   25

CHAPTER SIX   What God is Doing   29

Endnotes   35

About the Author

INTRODUCTION

It happened so quickly that few could have predicted it. Militant Sunni Jihadists burst clear from the confused morass of fighting in Syria to race across and claim large areas of neighboring Iraq. By 14 June 2014, the mostly Shi'ite army of Iraq in that area had collapsed. Having captured major northern Iraqi cities and threatening even the capital Baghdad, two weeks later Abu Bakr al–Husayni al–Baghdadi proclaimed himself as Caliph Ibrahim, "leader for Muslims everywhere".[1]

The Islamic State of Iraq and al Sham (ISIS) was renamed Islamic State (IS). By August 18 of that year it was estimated that 1.2 million people had been driven from their homes by an orgy of violence unleashed by IS.[2]

To mark the beginning of Ramadan, the Muslim month of fasting, the Caliph reportedly had proclaimed, "Fear Allah as he should be feared and do not die except as Muslims... Go forth, O mujahidin in the path of Allah. Terrify the enemies of Allah and seek death."[3] His troops, distinguishing themselves from Jabhat al–Nusra, their local al–Qaida opponents, would certainly obey their leader.

In the Ridda (Apostasy) Wars following the death of the Prophet Mohammad in 632, Muslims fought Muslims in a battle for supremacy. As each declared their opponent apostate, "tens of thousands of Arabs were burned, beheaded, dismembered or crucified."[4] The history of Muslim engagements is replete with such examples. No Muslim ruler is ever quarantined from the threat of apostasy.

A saying attributed to their Prophet Mohammad underscores the possibility:

"This umma (Islamic nation) of mine will split into seventy–three sects; one will be in paradise and seventy–two will be in hell."

When asked which sect was the true one, the prophet replied, 'al–jama'a', that is, the group which most literally follows the example or 'sunna' of Mohammad."[5]

As Mohammad's followers implement his example they fulfill a prophecy of another Prophet—Jesus—who said, "...all who draw the sword will die by the sword." (Matthew 26:52) Temporarily tensions regarding the existence of Israel are removed from media headlines to be replaced by a malignancy of Islamic violence which has metastasized leaving no region of the world uninfected.

How did this happen and how might Christians respond? Even more importantly, where is God in the midst of this seeming mess?

Read on.

CHAPTER ONE

No Compromise

On 8 August 2014, former head of the Australian Army, Lieutenant General Peter Leahy, reportedly said, "Australia is involved in the early stages of a war which is likely to last for the rest of the century." Michael Krause, a retired Major General, agreed. Aware of the army's experience in Iraq and Afghanistan he said, "I have seen these people. I know how they think. I know how they fight. There is no compromise possible."

The headline of *The Australian* newspaper the next day was, "We'll fight Islam (for) 100 years."[6] UK Prime Minister David Cameron reportedly made similar comments in the last week of August 2014.

In December 2014, the *New York Times* published comments made by General Michael K. Nagata, Special Operations commander for the United States in the Middle East. Commenting on the rise of the Islamic State (IS) he reportedly said,

> Whether we like it or not, we are all already involved because what is happening in the Middle East has global consequences.

"We have not defeated the idea. We do not even understand the idea."[7] At least he appreciated the obvious. What has been happening will not be defeated by military force alone. Whether we like it or not, we are all already involved because what is happening in the Middle East has global consequences.

When Western forces first entered Iraq and Afghanistan, a few observers said at the time that they would win some battles but would lose the war. In both those countries, no matter how political leaders reframe the outcomes, it may now be said that the losers by most measures have been Western nations. Little remains of their hoped–for outcomes from their interventions which cost trillions of dollars and thousands of lives.

Western democracies are unable to plan beyond their election cycle of 3–5 years. Muslim leaders think in terms of centuries. Islam's Prophet Mohammad invited Christian leaders of his time to submit to Islam. They declined. So Islamic forces determined to capture the Citadel of Christianity—Constantinople. Although their attacks were repeatedly repulsed, they finally succeeded after only 800 years.[8] Similar utterances were made against Rome. These have been renewed in recent times.

Islamic State spokesmen have been reported as saying, "We will conquer your Rome, break your crosses and enslave your women... If we do not reach that time, then our children and grandchildren will reach it and they will sell your sons as slaves at the slave market."[9] For activated Muslims the words and deeds of their Prophet Mohammad are not forgotten. No matter that some "prophecies" have not come to pass in the last fourteen centuries of Islam's existence. They are still to be pursued until achieved.

CHAPTER TWO

Gaza and Israel

In the Middle East if Jewish people are asked the basis of their claim to the land of Israel, the reply may be, "We have been here for 3000 years."

To the same question, people today called Palestinians may reply, "We have been here for 6000 years."

The same concept was humorously represented in an alleged encounter between Jewish and Palestinian negotiators who were meeting for the umpteenth time in a bid try to resolve the stalled peace process. On the appointed day before talks began, the Jewish team leader said, "We cannot start negotiations until we settle the matter of Moses' stolen clothes."

Sensing some sort of trap, the Palestinian team leader cautiously replied, "What do you mean Moses' stolen clothes?"

"Well," replied the Jewish leader, "when the children of Israel were travelling through the Sinai wilderness, Moses struck a rock and out gushed beautiful clear water to quench the thirst of the vast assembly. At that time Moses himself felt so hot he decided to take a dip in the new stream. So he took off his outer garments and went for a dip. But when he finished and went to get dressed his clothes were missing. Someone had stolen them. We will not proceed with further negotiations until we get them back."

The Palestinian negotiator was understandably outraged. "Why are you blaming us for this? There were no Palestinians around at that time!"

His Jewish counterpart instantly replied, "Precisely so. Now that we have settled that point, we can begin."

From the Biblical record we understand that God reserved for Abraham, Isaac, Jacob and their descendants a sliver of land on the coast along the Eastern Mediterranean seaboard. This became known as Israel—the Promised Land. The vast expanse of land to the east and south of Israel was reserved for the descendants of Ishmael, the first born son of Abraham by an Egyptian young woman, Hagar. She was a servant of Sarah, Abraham's wife. Sarah had given her to Abraham specifically for procreative purposes (Genesis 16). In time each group of descendants occupied their respective lands as prophesied.

In 1003 BC King David was at last able to conquer Jerusalem to make it his capital of undivided Israel. The area of the city at that that time was just 12 acres—a little less than 5 hectares. The rest of the Promised Land was conquered and possessed by King David except for the Philistine territory—today's Gaza. The people of this area were thought to be originally of Phoenician sea–faring origin.

What is happening today is not a new phenomenon.

Half a millennium later, in 586 BC, most of the people of what remained of Israel were deported as captives of war. They were taken to the vicinity of today's Baghdad. Towards the end of the sixth century BC, the deportees and their descendants were permitted to return to their homeland. The Jewish Temple in Jerusalem was rebuilt in 536–516 BC. Almost a further 70 years later, about 453 BC, Nehemiah arrived to rebuild the walls of Jerusalem.

Arabs and other local tribal chiefs, who were on the scene by that time, resisted his work. They ridiculed, threatened, concocted false reports and sought to terrorize the returnees. Their activities are recorded in the Bible in Nehemiah chapters 2, 4 and 6. What is happening today is not a new phenomenon. Jews remained in substantial possession of their land till 70 A.D. when the Romans destroyed the Jerusalem Temple and scattered the inhabitants.

> Today the spiritual descendants of Isaac and Ishmael face off against one another... irresistible force meets the immovable object.

Almost five and a half centuries later, in 638 AD, an Islamic Army captured Jerusalem for the first time. The city and its accompanying territory remained mostly under Muslim control thereafter. But the Jewish people did not vanish.

Jews were governing Jerusalem at the time of the Islamic invasion. Jewish Scribes were finalizing the text of Hebrew Bible during the seventh to eleventh centuries. With the rest of the population they endured the Crusades of the Middle Ages. They were still present in sufficient numbers in 1799 for Napoleon to invite them to form a state as the "Rightful Heirs of Palestine."[10]

However by the late 1800s, the brutality of the Ottoman Muslim authorities was so severe that many Jews were forced to flee.

Simultaneously the Ottoman government in Turkey began to repopulate the vacated land with Muslim refugees from other parts of their Empire in which there were disturbances.

In 1890 the Muslim population was only 432,000. By the time of modern Israel's establishment by the UN in 1947, the Muslim population, through Turkish repatriation policy, had almost tripled to 1,181,000.[11]

After 1918 with the defeat of the Turkish government in World War I, the Jewish population started to return. Many of them were fleeing from European threats and conflagrations, especially the later Holocaust of the 1940s, which saw an estimated six million Jews killed. Today the spiritual descendants of Isaac and Ishmael face off against one another as the proverbial irresistible force meets the immovable object.

Neither side in the current conflict is prepared to yield a centimeter of land. Article 7 in HAMAS's charter based on Islamic texts specifically asserts that they will destroy all Jews and Israel. The Palestinian Liberation Organization (PLO) was created in 1964. Its founding manifesto stated it was also formed "to attain the objective of liquidating Israel."[12]

Israel says, "If you attack we will retaliate."

HAMAS spokesman, Sami Abu Zuhri appeared on on Al–Aqsa television on 17 August 2014 and declared, "Our true war is not aimed at opening border crossings. It is aimed at the liberation of Jerusalem. We refuse to accept the continued defiling of our land by the occupier. The army of Mohammad has begun its return."[13] Neither HAMAS nor the PLO can accept the loss of territory once occupied by Muslim authorities. To them it remains a sacred trust, a Waqf, which must be regained.

The current off–again on–again war between Gaza and Israel has provided opportunity for mostly public pro–Palestinian reaction in many Western countries. In France, Germany, Italy, United Kingdom, USA, Australia and elsewhere, Muslims took to the streets showing a different side of Islam, reportedly shouting: "Heil Hitler. HAMAS HAMAS. Jews to the gas. We are all HAMAS. We are Jihad."[14] Many of those participating had been thought of as well–integrated, assimilated, moderate citizens who contributed to the rich mosaic of multiculturalism in those countries. In addition, many well–meaning non–Muslim sympathizers joined these processions.

In Sydney, Australia, as the crowd waved their black flags of jihad, the reported shout was:

Palestine is a Muslim land.

The solution is Jihad.

You can never stop Islam.

From Australia to Al Sham.

One Ummah (Muslim community) hand in hand

from Lakemba [a predominantly Muslim Sydney suburb] to Gaza.

One call—"Khalifa".[15]

The latest claimant for the role of Khalifa—the Caliph—is Abu Bakr al Baghdadi who claims to be the leader of international Islam and "Commander of the Faithful". On 5 July 2014, he spoke to the world from the "pulpit" of the great Mosque of al Nuri in the city of Mosul in Northern Iraq. He did so as Caliph, the first such since Mustafa Kemal Atatürk of Turkey dissolved the position in 1924.[16]

Later he would reportedly announce, "The long slumber of neglect has ended. The sun of Jihad has risen. Triumph looms on the horizon. Infidels are terrified. As East and West submit Muslims will own the earth."[17] His forces already controlled an area of territory greater than that of the UK. The movement's expansionary objectives were clear.

As for Israelis, the Muslim objectives about them are equally clear. In his Friday sermon on 22 August 2014 in Khan Younis in Gaza, Sheikh Mohammad Abu Rajab was reported as saying, "We pledged before the commanders of the Jihad to die for the sake of Allah; we have gathered the Zionists from all corners of the globe so that it will be easier to slaughter and kill them."[18]

The situation in Northern Syria and Iraq shares similarities.

CHAPTER THREE

Northern Syria and Iraq

In northern Syria and Iraq there are at least 18 different jihadi groups who seemingly have spent as much time fighting one another as they have fighting the Iran–supported Shi'ite surrogate regimes of President Bashar al–Assad in Syria and Prime Minister Haider al–Abadi in Iraq. Unleashed from the restraints imposed by dictators in those and other Middle Eastern countries, Jihadist groups rampaged across the land causing death and havoc wherever they went. They tortured, raped and killed adult non–Sunni males by beheading, crucifying and shooting. Reports say they raped and sold women, girls and boys into slavery, while saving some to gratify their own sexual desires.

In 2011 the US Commission on International Religious freedom noted: "The flight of Christians out of the region is unprecedented and it's increasing year by year." The city of Homs in Syria had a Christian population of 80 000 before jihadis arrived. In late 2012 it was reported that the last remaining Christian in the city had been murdered.[19]

In Iraq, Christians were 5% of the population but they have constituted 40% of the refugees fleeing Iraq. The head of the Chaldean Catholic Church in March 2013 reportedly said that in 2003 there were 300 churches in Iraq. A decade later there were only 50.[20]

On 6 June 2014 approximately 3000 jihadis overran the west bank of Mosul. As the capital of Nineveh Province in Northern Iraq it is the nation's second largest city. This province is the Arab–Kurd "fault line". It is also the homeland of Iraq's ancient indigenous Assyrian Christians.[21] Mosul had the highest concentration of Christians in Iraq.

Ultimately ISIS marked Christian homes with a red letter signifying "Nasrani", the Arabic word for Christian. These homes were later forfeited to the renamed IS. Christians fleeing toward Kurdistan were systematically robbed of all but the clothing they wore. Those who were identified as converts to Christianity were beheaded. In April 2015 Patriarch Kirill of Moscow and All Russia was reported as saying that, of the 45 churches in the city of Mosul, none remained. He added that, according to his estimate, 400 churches had been destroyed in Syria.[22]

In reponse to those who objected to the terror and what was happening, prominent writer and cleric, Hussein bin Mahmoud focused on just one methodology. He was reported as saying: "...beheading is an effective way to terrorize the enemies of Islam. Under Islamic law, American journalist James Foley was a Harbi, that is, a non–Muslim whose life was not protected by an agreement of protection. Islam allows and encourages such acts since it is a religion of war and fighting."[23]

Internationally prominent UK Muslim leader, Anjem Choudary, justified this particular beheading of American journalist, James Foley, by reportedly saying beheading was permissible under Sharia (Islamic) law. "Muslims who abide by Sharia and follow the jurisprudence do not make a distinction between civilian and army. This fellow was not just a civilian of America. He was a journalist."[24]

Even to question such actions from within the community may be dangerous. HAMAS in Gaza, like the movements in northern Iraq and Syria, is also known for its practice of extrajudicial execution. In the latter half of 2014 about 20 people were summarily executed and their bodies were dragged through the streets. Two of those executed were women. They had simply been asking questions about Palestinians who had been killed.[25]

When it comes to people like Yazidis and Shi'ites, they automatically qualify to be killed. Yazidis are regarded as infidels. Sunnis consider that Shi'ites are apostate because of their "innovations" such as shrine veneration and public self–flagellation—practices which have no Quranic support.

The Quran refers to Jews and Christians as "People of the Book". They are at least first invited to become Muslims. If they refuse they may be exiled, taxed into impoverishment or killed. For a detailed treatment of these practices see *The Third Choice* by Mark Durie.[26]

Muslims whom the West would have been regarded as moderates, reportedly suddenly turned on their Christian and other non–Muslim neighbors telling them to leave because these lands had become exclusively Muslim countries.[27] This occurred in communities where Muslims had lived in harmony with those of other religions for centuries. Assyrian

For the first time in 2000 years, Christianity has been all but obliterated from these lands.

Christians equated the situation with the genocide of a century ago when the Ottoman government was allegedly responsible for the deaths of more than 1.5 million Armenian and Christian groups that included Assyrians and Greeks.[28]

It was estimated that, by the end of 2014, 1.2 million people had been forced to flee. As in previous Muslim invasions, churches were destroyed or turned into mosques.

For the first time in 2000 years, Christianity has been all but obliterated from these lands.

But concerning these atrocities there have been few processions in the streets of Western cities. When movements like Boko Haram in Nigeria, Al Shebaab in Kenya and Somalia, the Muslim Brotherhood in Egypt, the governments of Sudan or Iran, repeatedly carry out their atrocities, there is little overseas public response.

Mehmet Gormez, the head of Turkey's religious affairs directorate, has claimed that each day an average of 1000 Muslims are killed worldwide and almost 90% are killed by other Muslims. If his estimate is accurate, this means that every four days the number of Muslims killed by other Muslims is more than those who have died in the last 10 years of the Israeli–Palestinian conflict.[29] Yet the Muslim community remains muted and silent in Western countries. It's only when Israel is involved that reaction is ramped up.

Archbishop Athanasius Toma Dewod of the Syrian Orthodox Church (UK) said, "They are killing our people in the name of Allah, telling people that anyone who kills a Christian will go straight to Paradise."[30]

There are many reasons that could be adduced by way of explanation for what is happening. Chief among them are interpretations and applications of Islamic theology and Western democratic practices.

CHAPTER FOUR

Why is This Happening?

First, there is the teaching of Islam.

Muslims are not our enemies. Like people anywhere they hold many different opinions. As individuals they mostly desire peaceful lives and security for home and family.

The real threat is Islam itself. Its teaching is contained in:

(a) The Quran, which is claimed to be direct revelation from Allah through his Prophet Mohammad.

(b) The Traditions (Hadith) of which there are many thousands. These tell us what Islam's Prophet said and did.

(c) The Life of Mohammad (Sirat Rasul Allah) by Ibn Ishaq written in 767 AD, a century after Mohammad's death.

(d) Codified collections of material that became Sharia Law.

Whatever is found in these volumes validates or authenticates Muslim belief and practice. There seems to be nothing in the

> Reform of Islam
> becomes mostly
> a Westernized
> vain hope.

current revivalist upsurge of Islam around the world which cannot be sourced, either in example or motivation, somewhere in these books. Variant interpretations of this body of literature sacred to Islam were closed a millennium ago. At that time Muslim scholars turned away from the processes of philosophy and rational thought and took refuge in dogma.

One of Islam's greatest mediaeval scholars, al Ghazali, declared the gate of ijtihad was closed and "since then Sunni Islam has adopted the official position that no new interpretations of the law can be entertained."[31] Therefore reform of Islam becomes mostly a Westernized vain hope.

So, it is taught that Muslims are the best people on earth, that they will rule the whole world, that they are winners and all others are losers (Q24:52;3:85;39:65) and that once Muslims have conquered a country, it is theirs forever.

When these aspirations are frustrated, zealous and revolutionary reformers within Islam arise and declare that Muslim people have become nominal and apostate. Allah's will is thwarted. Regaining his blessing will only happen if all return to the basics, to resume jihad against the infidels and against Muslim rulers who have compromised the true Way, the Sunnah.

The siren call to reform Islam—by returning to its earliest practices—becomes a compelling solution to the question that bedevils all Muslim societies, "How should we live?"

The former Kuwaiti minister of information, Saad bin Tafla al Ajami, summed up what is happening thus: "The truth that we cannot deny is: ISIS learned from our schools, prayed in our mosques, listened to our media and our religious platforms, read from our books and references, and followed fatwas (religious edicts) we produced."[32] Precisely so.

No Muslim wants to criticize another Muslim who longs to return to Islam as practiced and exemplified by Mohammad. To do so would risk being in contravention of Islam's sacred texts. This attitude is so especially if Muslims are in a minority in a non–Muslim country. Thus when the New York Towers were destroyed, there was muted reaction by Muslims in the West. But in many Muslim majority cities there was distribution of sweets and dancing in the streets.

The second major reason revivalist Islam is running rampant in the Middle East and increasingly behaving as it does in the West is Western Democratic "leadership".

Western Democracy

Nearly all politicians want to retain personal power more than anything else. In a democracy winning votes does this. Votes are won by keeping electors happy by giving them what they want even if this is not in the best long term interests of the nation.

In the case of Australia, reportedly after careful investigation, the Department of Immigration under a Hawke Labor government issued a deportation order for Sheik Taj El Din Hamid Hilaly for anti–Semitic activities. But he lived in Lakemba, a suburb of Sydney, where there were lots of votes by Muslims. So the Hawke government overturned its own Department's edict. As Grand Mufti, leader of Muslims in Australia, Imam Hilaly would later reportedly describe the New York atrocity as "God's work against infidels". Later still when Muslim young men were convicted of raping non–Muslim women, reportedly Hilaly's response was that the women got what they deserved because of the way in which they dressed.

In the 20 Federal Parliamentary seats in western Sydney, many have significant Muslim populations. The Labor party holds 19 of these. When the former Foreign Minister Bob Carr reportedly spent an hour with then Prime Minister Gillard prior to the federal election of 2013, emphasizing the importance of the Muslim vote, the Gillard Labor government dropped support for Israel in the United Nations.[33]

The Abbot Liberal National coalition government in August 2014 came under pressure from the Muslim community and others. As a result, it dropped its intention to change section 18(c) of the Federal Racial Discrimination Act which some had claimed significantly restricted freedom of speech. The government hoped, that in so doing, it would gain Muslim support for its proposal to enact tougher anti–terrorism laws. Muslims leaders approved the first Government's action but opposed the second.

Democratically elected governments seldom do anything that may risk votes at the next election. This pattern is repeated in most Western democracies.

An election in the autonomous region of Catalonia in Spain was due in 2014. 465,000 Muslims live in that region. Their leaders reported that the government, the Convergence and Union Party, had promised permission to build the third largest mosque in the world financed from Qatar, if the Muslims voted for them. The mosque's minaret was planned to tower 300 metres to overshadow symbolically the spires of the Sagardia Familia Roman Catholic cathedral by 130 metres. In one of the mosques in that region, Abdelwahab Houzi preached in support of voting for the Convergence party saying that it would represent a significant step in Muslims accumulating power with a view to implementing Sharia Law.[34]

In spite of atrocities in early 2015 in Australia, France, Denmark and the Middle East, all perpetrated by committed Muslims,

USA President Barack Obama continued to be reported as reassuring his nation that ISIS was not Islamic. "Their actions represent no faith, least of all the Muslim faith." His Secretary of State, John Kerry, was similarly reported as saying ISIS was only "masquerading as a religious movement [which] has nothing to do with Islam." Throughout the duration of its terms in office the Obama administration resolutely refused to link any Jihadi terrorism with anything remotely connected to Islam.

UK Prime Minister, David Cameron, was of the view that the recurrent violence "abuses and perverts Islam." Former UK Home Secretary, Jack Straw, insisted that what was happening was "completely contrary to Islam." French President, Francois Hollande, was reported as saying that the assailants of the Charlie Hebdo and Hyper Cacher massacres had "nothing to do with the Muslim faith." French minister Thierry Mandon even recommended building more mosques as a counter to radicalization![35] Japanese Prime Minister, Shinzo Abe, is on the record as saying, "Extremism and Islam are completely different things."[36] Many other Western political leaders have said similar things, all of which overlook the teaching and commands in Islam's sacred texts and the well–documented history of its religious military imperialism. Obvious truth is sacrificed on the altar of political expediency to garner as many Muslim votes as possible at their respective next elections.

These leaders declared that those who carry out such actions are not true Muslims who are mostly "moderate". But who is a true "moderate"? As Tarek Fatah notes, "The same men and women who

Western secular politicians continue to fail to engage the theology of Islam that undergirds what is happening.

spout hate, masquerade as 'moderate' Muslims and sprinkle just enough words about 'multiculturalism', 'charter rights' and 'pluralism' to fool many."[37]

In effect Western leaders in their manipulative ignorance say that "extremists" are apostates and therefore unrepresentative of "peaceful Islam". For non–Muslims to declare who is a true Muslim and who has become apostate, a process known as takfir, causes mirth among jihadists. One reportedly tweeted that this is equivalent to "a pig covered in faeces giving hygiene advice to others."[38]

Western secular politicians continue to fail to engage the theology of Islam that undergirds what is happening. They therefore misunderstand cause and effect. By definition they continue even to disallow theology in public debate. World-renowned secularist sociologist, Peter Berger, said, "Those who neglect religion in their analyses of contemporary affairs do so at great peril."[39]

What has happened in the West as political leaders urge all to put their heads in the sand with them was pictorially well-represented in two pages of Australia's only national newspaper on 10 March 2015. On page 13 there was a large photograph accompanying a full page report on how Islamic State (IS) had obtained the committed allegiance of Jund al–Kalifah in Algeria, black–clad fighters in Afghanistan, a surge of recruits from Tunisia, groups supporting the movement in Pakistan, similar support in Libya, Al–Qaida in the Arabian Peninsula (AQAP) in Yemen, Ansar Bayt al–Maqdis in Egypt, Jamaah Islamihya in Indonesia, Boko Haram in West Africa and their troops in Syria and Iraq.[40]

On the opposite page 12 of the same newspaper there was a series of colorful photographs of the Chelsea Flower Show (UK) and a large tourist vessel sailing down the Rhine between flower–filled banks. The accompanying article was entitled "Earthly Delights".[41] The assumption could be drawn that these two worlds so far apart were never meant to meet.

Unfortunately with 26236 documented deadly Muslim terrorist attacks affecting countless millions of people across the world in the period 11 September 2011–28 June 2015,[42] these worlds have already collided. As classic Islamic theology mandates, Dar al–Islam (the House of Islam) must prosecute Jihad against Dar al–Harb (the House of War, in which the infidels live) until they conquer all and rule the world, or else until the Islamic version of Jesus returns to smash all crosses, kill all pigs and cause all non–Muslims to revert to Islam or be exterminated.

As Christians swirling in the vortex of this super–heated cauldron of conflict and confusion, how do we respond?

CHAPTER FIVE

Our Response

In each of the Gospels there is a record of what happened when armed men came to arrest Jesus. The Apostle Peter's natural reaction was to counter violence with violence. He struck out and wounded a soldier with a sword. Jesus would have none of it. (John 18:10-11) He healed the wounded man (Luke 22:51) and forbade such responses. As Muslims follow the oft times violent and military example of their Prophet, Christians are obliged to follow that of Jesus. It may be difficult but Jesus never gave easy options. Some of these are as follow:

1) Reject all personal violence, hatred and political triumphalism

Six centuries before Mohammad, followers of Jesus attempted to make him king. He rejected their political invitation, journeyed from Galilee to Jerusalem and accepted crucifixion.[43] As Mohammad is the example of the perfect man for Muslims (Q.33:21; 53:1–3), Jesus is the model for Christians. "Let us fix our eyes on Jesus the author and perfecter of our faith." (Hebrews 12:2)

Responses of armed resistance are matters for governments to decide as they exercise their responsibility in protecting people. (Romans 13:1–7)

2) Refuse to fear

That is what Islamic terrorism tries to produce (Q6:80). We live by faith, not fear. Jesus said, "I tell you, My friends, do not be afraid of those who kill the body and after that can do no more... Fear him who, after killing the body, has power to throw you into hell." (Luke 12:4–5)

God is still in control. If we have read the Bible, we already know how all this will end. FEAR is False Evidence Appearing Real. It corrodes confidence in God's goodness, causing an early onset of spiritual dementia deleting memory of what God has already done for us. 21 times in the Gospels, Jesus says, "Don't be afraid," "Fear not," or "Have courage."

3) Develop friendships with Muslims

Don't hate them to death. Love them to life. It's not their fault that they have been coercively and collectively persuaded into believing what, from a Christian perspective, is a cosmic deception.

4) Share generously

Give to Christian agencies that are working in the current refugee crises and in the various theatres of conflict.

5) Offer hospitality

Be ready to offer hospitality to any real refugees from these crises. "Do not forget to entertain strangers..." (Hebrews 13:2)

6) Persevere in persistent prayer

"Though we live in the world, we do not wage war as the world does. The weapons we fight with are not the weapons of the world. On the contrary they have divine power to demolish strongholds... Take captive every thought to make it obedient to Christ." (2 Corinthians 10:3–5)

Prayer is the pivot on which the world turns. Further information and help can be found in the Religious Liberty Prayer Bulletin[44] and through the book, *Turn Back the Battle: Isaiah Speaks to Christians Today* by Elizabeth Kendal.[45]

7) Always commend Jesus

Walk the talk with words and deeds, always asking, what would Jesus do? If you do, amazing things may happen. You may discover what God is doing.

CHAPTER SIX

What God is Doing

Undoubtedly God grieves to see what is happening. But he is not inactive.

In the city of Melbourne in March 2015 an amazing celebratory funeral took place. Ahmed[46] had died after a long struggle with cancer. Four days before his death, his mother arrived completely shrouded in dress demanded in Middle Eastern Muslim countries. After Ahmed's death she spoke at his funeral.

She spoke of the great disappointment her son had been to the family, given his lack of achievement and direction as well as dangerous habits which had ensnared him. His departure to Australia added insult to injury. Upon her arrival she was amazed to see her son completely transformed. He was now a man greatly honored by the many people who came to farewell him before he died. He had become a leader in a faith community of followers of Jesus. This had occurred when he met with a group of people who lived the responses previously listed.

> Muslims are tired of Muslims killing Muslims. They are looking for real peace.

Now, in his home, in spite of the ravages of cancer and imminent physical death, there was peace, joy and confidence in what Jesus had accomplished for all who would follow Him.

Ahmed's mother was so impacted by what she saw that she discarded her regulation Islamic covering, gave her prayer beads and prayer mat to others to destroy. She gave instructions that, back home in their country of origin, the memorial event must not be one of grief, weeping and sadness. It was to be a time of joy and celebration. The son which had been lost had been found. She was determined to encounter the Son whom Ahmed had discovered and also to join a group of like-minded believers upon return to her country.

In the troubled areas of Iraq and Syria today, church planting has reportedly accelerated 5 to 10 times what it was previously. Syrian refugees in Lebanese refugee camps are also becoming Christians.[47] Muslims are tired of Muslims killing Muslims. They are looking for real peace, not the mirage of peace that apocalyptic Islam proclaims.

One former foot soldier recently put it like this: "I have been a man of violence. I was a jihadist. But I observed that violence only begets violence. In my search for another way I met Jesus. He has transformed me. He is peace."[48]

In another area of Muslim dominance, former violent jihadists have become the best Christian evangelists. Authorities are reluctant to send them to prison because that results in many other inmates becoming followers of Jesus.[49]

"...the law was given through Moses; grace and truth came through Jesus Christ." (John 1:17)

Muslims consider themselves the slaves of Allah as well as the harsh Law formulated in the name of this unknowable spiritual entity. People tend to become like the God they worship.

Jesus Christ fulfilled the demands of the law and freed us for a relationship with a loving Heavenly Father. Our Muslim brothers and sisters are in need of that same deliverance more than ever. The process can be quite dramatic.

"Padina" lives in the Middle East. As a child she learned to pray five times a day. She also memorized significant portions of the Quran. She hated Christians and rejoiced whenever she heard about Christians being persecuted. She had been taught that Muslims who killed Christians would automatically earn admission to Paradise. She strove hard to follow every rule of Islam. When she prayed, she was scrupulous. If she thought she had not prepared precisely by washing in the prescribed manner, she would rewash and recommence the prayer.

Padina became very depressed and suicidal. In spite of her best efforts she felt so distant from Allah. Her bedridden, partially paralysed mother was dying with a very aggressive form of Muscular Sclerosis.

Padina decided the only option to end her own misery was to commit suicide. When she informed her mother of her intention, her mother asked that she be assisted to die at the same time.

As the ladies prepared for their final hours on earth they turned on the television. A Christian pastor was on air: "If you are hopeless, oppressed and planning to commit suicide the Lord says, 'Stop.' He has a hope and a future for you. If you are planning to kill yourself stop and call me."

Padina's mother phoned in. For thirty minutes she spoke with the preacher. All the while her daughter was saying, "I'm going to do this. Nothing is going to stop me tonight."

Then she heard her mother uttering a prayer of repentance seeking salvation. Padina was furious. "Why in the last seconds of your life are you doing this? Now you are going to hell."

Padina's mother begged her to speak to the television preacher. But Padina's angry response was hardly encouraging. "Jesus can do nothing! Jesus is nothing! I will not blaspheme Mohammad by speaking to this infidel." But finally she took the phone and spoke to the man on the other end in a frighteningly cold tone. She reiterated that she intended to kill herself and that Jesus could do nothing for them. For an hour she argued, "I just want to die."

The preacher reminded her, "You said it yourself. Allah has done nothing for you. Give Jesus just one chance. You can always kill yourself next week."

When this challenge was given, Padina thought that this was the best way she could serve Allah one last time before committing suicide. She agreed she would pray for a week. If Jesus had not done anything by then she would call in and she would kill herself live on air as everyone listened in. This would enable her to say to Allah, "Even taking my life was for you."

Early the next morning Padina was awakened by a sound. She got up and found her mother walking perfectly. The two women immediately hastened to the hospital. The medical staff examined blood tests and an MRI scan after which they declared, "This is a miracle. There is no sign of MS in her body."

Padina insisted that something must be wrong. The medical staff was equally insistent that nothing was wrong. The doctors exclaimed, "This is a miracle. To what Imam did you pray?"

Padina replied, "It wasn't an Imam. It was Jesus."

Later on Padina said, "When I spoke those words my heart changed. I told Jesus, 'You are the living God. You cleansed me and filled me. I'll give up my life for you.'"

Today Padina and her mother are apostates from Islam. This offense is punishable by death. They risk their lives ministering in their country leading a movement of thousands of new disciples of Jesus.[50]

Elias is a Christian worker. He lived among Somali Muslim refugees. One night, as he was preparing to eat his evening meal alone, there was a knock on his door. Outside stood a 65 year–old Somali from war–torn Mogadishu. This was Sheikh Abdul–Ahad. Elias nervously wondered if this terrorist leader had come to kill him.

Without any formal greeting the Sheikh suddenly spoke. "Did the blood of Jesus pay for the sins of everyone in the world? Answer me—yes or no?"

Elias answered, "Yes."

Immediately the Sheikh shouted, "You're lying. The blood of Jesus cannot forgive my sins!"

Then he told Elias of all the violent things he had done in his life. As he began to tremble and weep he cried out, "I need relief and forgiveness for all that."

Elias said, "If you and I tonight agree to pray and ask God, He will answer your prayers."

Somewhere between 2 and 7 million Muslims have come to Christ. The harvest is ready. God is moving.

That night as they prayed the old Sheikh received Jesus and was saved. Before he left he grasped Elias and said, "When you look at me on the street, you see me in my Muslim clothing with my big beard and you are afraid. I tell you the truth: we dress this way to make you afraid of us. Don't be afraid. You need to know that inside we are empty. We need the Gospel of Jesus."[51]

Before this century there were very few converts from Islam to Christianity during Islam's fourteen centuries of existence. But today it is estimated at least 70 movements underway in 29 nations account for somewhere between 2 and 7 million Muslims who have come to Christ.[52]

The harvest is ready. God is moving. The question is, are we ready and courageous enough to move with him to bring in a mighty harvest, the like of which has never before been seen in human history?

ENDNOTES

1. Tom Coghlan, Deborah Haynes, *Militants declare Islamic Caliphate.* The Australian, July 1 2014, 7.

2. Hala Jaber, Tony Harden, *Yazidis still fear genocide as US vacillates. The Australian*, August 18 2014, 6.

3. Aymenn Jawad al-Tamimi, *Abu Bakr al=Baghdadi's Message as Caliiph*, http://www.gatestoneinstitute.org/4387/baghdadi-isis-caliphate, July 2 2014.

4. www.raymondibrahim.com/islam/living-and-dying-by-the-sword-of-jihad/ February 19 2015

5. www.raymondibrahim.com/islam/living-and-dying-by-the-sword-of-jihad/ (sighted February 19 2015)

6. Brendan Nicholson, *We'll fight Islam 100 years.* The Weekend Australian, August 9-10 2014, 1.

7. Graham Wood, *What ISIS Really Wants*, March 2015, 1. http://www.theatlantic.com/features/archive/2015/02/what-isis-really-wants/384980/

8. http://www.raymondibrahim.com/islam/the-siege-of-constantinople/ (viewed August 16 2014)

9. Graham Wood, *What ISIS Really Wants*, March 2015, 7. http://www.theatlantic.com/features/archive/2015/02/what-isis-really-wants/384980/

10. George Phillips, *A British Conference on Israel's Right to Exist: Really?* http://www.gatestoneinstitute.org/5534/israel-right-to-exist-conference. April 12, 2015.

11. Ezequiel Doiny, *The Muslim Colonists: Forgotten Facts about the Arab-Israeli Conflict.* http://www.gatestoneinstitute.org/4611/muslim-colonists. August 15 2014.

12. Israel and Judaism Studies, *Creation, aims, methods and effectiveness of the Palestinian Liberation Organisation (PLO) 1964-1974.* www.ijs.org.au/The-Palestine-Liberation-Organisation/default.aspx (sighted April 17, 2015).

13. MEMRI TV, *Hamas Spokesman: Our War Is For Liberation of Jerusalem Not For Lifting Of Blockade.* Viewed August 26 2014.

14. Denis MacEoin, *The New Romantics 'Being Fair' to Terrorist Groups*. http://www.gatestoneinstitute.org/4602/new-romantics. August 14 2014.

15. Andrew Bolt, *Wake up Labor, smell the threat*. HeraldSun, August 4 2014, 13.

16. Graham Wood, *What ISIS Really Wants*, March 2015, 1. http://www.theatlantic.com/features/archive/2015/02/ what-isis-really-wants/384980/

17. Daniel Pipes, *Caliph Ibrahim's Brutal Moment*. The Washington Times. http://www.danielpipes.org/14691/caliph-ibrahim August 5 2014.

18. www.memri.org/clip/en/4442.htm, August 22 2014, viewed August 29 2014.

19. http://www.raymondibrahim.com/muslim-persecution-of-christians/ world-ignores-christian-exodus-from-islamic-world/ August 8 2014.

20. Quoted by Robert Spencer, www.jihadwatch.org/2013/03/myjihad-in-iraq-only-57-churches-left-in-the-entire-country.html.

21. http://elizabethkendal.blogspot.com/2014/06/isis-takes-war-back-to-iraq.html. July 1 2014.

22. http://www.raymondibrahim.com/muslim-persecution-of-christians/400-syrian-churches-destroyed-christianity-nearing-extinction-in-mideast-russian-orthodox-patriarch/ April 17 2015.

23. *Jihadi Cleric Justifies IS Beheadings: Islam Is a Religion Of Beheading*. MEMRI Special Despatch/5826/August 25 2014.

24. Ryan Mauro, www.clarionproject.org/print/analysis/uks-anjem-choudary-justifies-beheading-of-james-foley (viewed August 30 2014).

25. Khaled Abu Toameh, http://www.gatestoneinstitute.org/4646/ hamas-war-crimes. August 25 2014.

26. Mark Durie, *The Third Choice*, Deror Books, 2010.

27. MEMRI Daily, Special Dispatch No.5820, August 13 2014.

28. Rachel Baxendale, *Churches demand safe haven for Christians*. The Australian, August 25 2014, 2.

29. Sam Westrop, http://www.clarionproject.org/print/analysis/ uk-islamists-join-neo-nazis-marxists-anti-semitism (viewed August 28 2014).

30. Elizabeth Kendall, *Religious Liberty Prayer Bulleting, 273*. August 13 2014.

31. Robert A. Reilly, *The Closing of the Muslim Mind*. ISI Books, Wilmington, Delaware, 2011, x-xi.

32. Quotable Quotes, The Clarion Project (Radicalislam.org). Issue 128. August 21 2014 (viewed August 22 2014].

33. Andrew Bolt, *We're muzzled, but bigots rant*. Herald Sun, August 17 2014, 13.

34. Soeren Kern, http://www.clarionproject.org/print/analysis/ barcelona-mega-mosque-promised-separatists-votes (viewed August 17 2014).

35. Jennifer Oriel, *Political Correctness Shackles the War on Terror*. The Australian, April 14, 2015, 12.

36. Daniel Pipes, *Why Politicians Pretend Islam Has No Role in Violence*, The Washington Times, March 9 2015. http://danielpipes.org/15618/ islam-violence.

37. Tarek Fatah, *The "Shockingly Anti-Western Views" of Supposed Moderates*, http://www.clarionproject.org/blog/canada/ shockingly-anti-western-views-many-moderates.

38. Graham Wood, *What ISIS Really Wants*, March 2015, 20. http://www.theatlantic.com/features/archive/2015/02/ what-isis-really-wants/384980/

39. Bernard Lane, *Academic looks for theoretical salvation*. The Australian, August 27 2014, 28.

40. Bruce Loudon, *Terror's Unholy Alliance*, The Australian, March 10, 2015, 13.

41. Susan Kurosawa, *Earthly Delights*, The Australian, March, 12.

42. www.thereligionofpeace.com, sighted June 28 2015.

43. Jonathan Borman, *Confessing the Peace of Jesus in a Terroristic World*. A Statement and Appeal by EMM Christian/Muslim Relations Team. n.d.

44. http://rlprayerbulletin.blogspot.com.au/

45. Elizabeth Kendal. *Turn Back the Battle: Isaiah Speaks to Christians Today*, Deror Books, Melbourne, 2012.

46. Name changed and country of origin withheld.

47. Source withheld.

48. Source withheld.

49. Source withheld.

50. Catalyticministries.com/Padina/

51. David Garrison, *A Wind in the House of Islam*, Wigtake Resources, Monument, CO, 2014, 80-81.

52. Ibid, 5.s

ABOUT THE AUTHOR

Dr Stuart Robinson is the Founding Pastor of Australia's largest Baptist Church. Before that he worked for fourteen years in South Asia where he pioneered church planting among Muslims. He travels extensively as a speaker at Seminars and Conferences. He is the author of ten books including best selling titles, *Mosques & Miracles, Defying Death, The Prayer of Obedience* and *The Challenge of Islam*. He graduated from four tertiary institutions. Stuart was born in Brisbane and is married to Margaret. They have three married children.

www.ingramcontent.com/pod-product-compliance
Lightning Source LLC
Chambersburg PA
CBHW060042040426
42331CB00032B/2235